Gardiner Spring

State thanksgiving during the rebellion

Gardiner Spring

State thanksgiving during the rebellion

ISBN/EAN: 9783337207861

Printed in Europe, USA, Canada, Australia, Japan

Cover: Foto ©ninafisch / pixelio.de

More available books at **www.hansebooks.com**

State Thanksgiving during the Rebellion.

A SERMON,

PREACHED NOVEMBER 28, 1861,

BY

GARDINER SPRING, D.D.,

PASTOR OF THE BRICK PRESBYTERIAN CHURCH IN THE CITY OF NEW YORK.

NEW YORK:

HARPER & BROTHERS, PUBLISHERS,

FRANKLIN SQUARE.

1862.

THANKSGIVING SERMON.

"Thus saith the Lord, Let not the wise man glory in his wisdom, neither let the mighty man glory in his might, let not the rich man glory in his riches; but let him that glorieth glory in this, that he understandeth and knoweth me, that I am the Lord which exercise loving-kindness, judgment, and righteousness in the earth; for in these things I delight, saith the Lord."—*Jeremiah*, ix., 23, 24.

It is an affecting, a bitter lamentation, which introduces the chapter that contains this wholesome admonition. The prophet who uttered it was a devout and strong patriot; and though he foresaw the calamities that were coming upon his country, and was promised security and plenty if he would renounce his allegiance and go over to the enemy, he chose rather to share her disasters. Her wickedness had provoked the God of Israel; the measure of it was full, and wrath was about to fall upon them to the uttermost, in the destruction of their city, and in the exile and dispersion of the highly-favored and sig-

nally-punished people. The weeping prophet was worn out with sorrow; their sins and
desolations had well-nigh exhausted his griefs,
and he exclaims, "O that my head were waters, and mine eyes a fountain of tears, that I
might weep day and night for the slain of the
daughter of my people!" In the midst of all
these visitations they were a proud and self-
glorying nation. Their history was little else
than the narrative of their progress and splen-
dor; and it was to the last degree difficult to
persuade them that the land once so pre-emi-
nent in arms and physical resources would be
the prey of a foreign power; once so distinguished for its luxuriant fertility should ever
become "a desolation, and an astonishment,
and a curse." Among other sins, therefore,
the prophet was directed to rebuke their national egotism and vanity. The pre-eminence
they had gained they felt *wise* enough, and
strong enough, and *wealthy* enough **to** defend and maintain.

The thoughts suggested on the present occasion must necessarily be modified by events
that are passing around us. The melancholy
conflict in which we are engaged is full of
danger; we need the shield and buckler of an

Almighty arm. If we fail to honor the God
of heaven and earth; if our rulers, our warriors, our churches and their ministers lose
sight of their dependence on Him; and if we
boast of our wisdom, our martial prowess, and
our wealth, we may well despair of the restored integrity and permanent peace and
prosperity of our beloved land. The text
specifies those things in which we may* *not*
glory and those in which we *may* glory. Let
us advert,

I. In the first place, TO THOSE NATIONAL
QUALIFICATIONS AND ATTAINMENTS IN WHICH
WE MAY NOT GLORY.

LET NOT THE WISE MAN GLORY IN HIS WIS-
DOM. This was the marked characteristic
of ancient Israel. With all their faults, they
were among the wisest nations of the earth;
their history, their laws, and institutions placed
them upon an eminence far above the con-
temporaneous and surrounding nations. The
superiority of ancient Greece and Rome over
less intellectual and less cultivated lands, and
the superiority of Great Britain and France
over all the nations in the north of Europe,
and the superiority of the American States
over the Red Men of the forest, are to be

attributed to their intellectual advancement.
Men and nations obtain credit and distinction
for nothing more than their wisdom. Gath-
ered up as it is from habits of thought and
study, from careful observation, and, not un-
frequently, painful experience, it is no matter
of wonder that it is highly esteemed. How
to devise their plans for the present and the
future ; how to adjust them in view of the facilities that may advance, or obstacles which
may oppose their progress ; how to form a cor-
rect judgment of the character and tactics of
friends and foes; how to anticipate, and fore-
stall, and frustrate evil machinations and turn
them to good account ; how to act so as to
hazard nothing by rashness and lose nothing
by delay ; how, in few words, to select the best
ends, and the best time and means of accomplishing them, is a rare faculty when bestowed,
and a rare attainment when sought after.

We have high authority for saying, "Wisdom is better than weapons of war." Yet
much as we should seek its counsels, and
profitable as it is to direct, we may not make
it the ground of our dependence or the foun-
dation of our hopes. God gave the Assyrian
his ascendency over the nations, and his tri-

umphs upon Mount Zion and in Jerusalem; and in the pride of his heart he said, "I have done it by *my wisdom;* for I am prudent, and I have removed the bounds of the people, and mine hand hath found as a nest their riches." But God rebuked his arrogance, and brought down his stout heart, "as when a standard-bearer fainteth." No nation on the earth has gloried more in its wisdom than this young republic. Our national independence, our noble Constitution, our transactions with foreign governments, we have attributed to the wisdom of our fathers, to the far-sightedness of our politicians, and to the skill of our statesmen; and for our safety as a nation we have self-complacently relied upon the intelligence of the people.

We may well be thankful for these attainments as God's agents in the achievement of his own wise and benevolent ends, but we may not *glory* in them. We honor the wisdom and generalship of the warrior, but there is a wisdom above him that "taketh the wise in their own craftiness." There is "no wisdom nor counsel against the Lord." Our wisdom will fail us, and the "prudence of our wise men will perish" if we idolize the creature. "God will destroy the wisdom of the wise, and bring to naught the understanding of the prudent." Let not the wise glory in their wisdom!

NEITHER LET THE MIGHTY MAN GLORY IN HIS MIGHT.

The boastful remark has been often repeated, that this fearful contest must be decided by the superiority of numbers and physical force. It would seem so: I hope in God it will prove so. A disciplined army of 600,000, weekly augmented by such large accessions, would seem to give little hope to the rebellion, but rather justify the American people in strong anticipations of victory. Nor are such anticipations to be discouraged or frowned upon so long as they are modified by humble reverence of the Deity, and a chastened dependence upon his providence. Human dependence and human activity stand abreast in all the arrangements of the divine government. God has his own way of working, but it is well-nigh uniformly through human instrumentality. In repelling the invasions of this rebellion, our common sense and common Christianity teach us to make a due estimate of our numbers. "What king," says the Savior, "going to make war against another king, sitteth not down first and consulteth whether he be able, with 10,000, to meet him that cometh against him with 20,000 ?" We do no honor to the providence of God by listlessness and inactivity ; rather do we dishonor it when we hesitate to put forth those exertions by which we become "fellow-workers with him," and do homage to it only when our co-operation helps forward his designs.

Yet, while the Creator condescends to assign to his creatures their proper place and instrumentality, it becomes the creature to recognize and honor the supremacy of the Almighty Creator. Though the spirit of the warrior may be stirred within him, and he put forth his most ardent zeal and intense activity, "the mighty man MAY NOT GLORY in his might." The race is not always to the swift, nor the battle to the strong. Opportunity and a particular providence—"time and chance happeneth to them all." Jonathan and his armor-bearer achieved more than the whole army of Saul. The 300 that lapped under Gideon were more potent than the combined forces of Midian and Amalek. The sling and the stone of David subdued the impious and

vaunting champion of the Philistines. When
Israel trembled before the hosts of Syria, and
cast themselves at the foot of God's throne, a
sweeping pestilence destroyed 185,000 of their
enemies in a single night. A blasting storm
scattered the naval power of Spain on the
very eve of her anticipated glorying in England's downfall. When Louis XIV. entered
the Low Countries with an army that threat-
ened to bear down all opposition, a few undis-
ciplined troops, with the Prince of Orange at
their head, opened the channels for the ocean
to inundate their island city, and their proud
foe was disheartened. When Leopold of Austria marched against the cantons of Switzer-
land with an army of 20,000 men, the patriotic
Swiss, with an army of 1400, and with the loss
of fourteen men, either killed or dispersed the
whole Austrian forces. Frederick the Great
of Prussia, in the terrible campaign of 1757,
with an army of 260,000 men, stood against
the combined powers of France, Austria, Rus-
sia, and Sweden, who brought into the field an
army of 700,000. England, during the war
of the Revolution, counted on her armies and
her navy to overthrow this American republic; but there were causes above her boasted

prowess, and she saw the "little one become a thousand, and the small one a strong nation." Napoleon once said that "he had found that Providence always favored the strongest battalions." Yet he did not find it so in the Russian campaign. He could contend with serried hosts, but he could not contend with the elements. He could contend with men ; but, be the numbers and discipline of his army what they might, he could not contend with storms, and pestilence, and God Almighty. This is the lesson which the brave and the mighty are slow to learn. At his bidding who works and none shall let it, and out of whose hand none can deliver—even without the aid of second causes, the foreseeing may become blind, the reflecting and considerate may become precipitate and rash, the brave and the mighty may become panic-struck, may mistake friend for foe, and flee from the field when there are none to pursue them. This generous flame may not always burn in the hour of alarm. This contempt of danger may veil its intrepid front amid blood and carnage. I have no such confidence in the prowess of the mighty as to be persuaded that, by many an unthought-of incident, the God of heaven may not disappoint the warrior's anticipations, make his face gather paleness, and turn his proud hopes into humiliation and despair. We honor his martial spirit, but we would rebuke his arrogance and pride. We admire his tranquil courage amid convulsive agonies and slaughtered corpses, and yet we say, "Let not the mighty man glory in his might."

Once more: NEITHER LET THE RICH MAN GLORY IN HIS RICHES. That "money is the sinews of war" is a maxim as old as the days of Dryden. That nation is infatuated who, in this, as well as in every other view, does not "count the cost" of its battles. Most cheerfully have our loyal states, our moneyed institutions, and our rich men poured forth their treasures for the suppression of this rebellion; and most gladly do poorer men, so far from regarding the legal demands of the government an uncalled-for exaction, yield it the support of their hard-earned stipend. This is right, and just as it should be. Yet when I hear the remark often repeated that the nation is *sure* to come off victorious *which has the longest purse*, and listen to it clothed in "great swelling words of vanity," I confess to some misgivings as to the result of this vain boasting. I am afraid God will frown upon us.

These loyal states have acquired wealth, sometimes dishonestly and wickedly, but for the most part by honest industry, severe economy, useful arts and inventions, and therefore we glory in it. We have repudiated the aristocracy of hereditary descent, and hereditary place and titles, but we are no strangers to the aristocracy of wealth. With gratitude to the Father of lights, we acknowledge we are a rich nation. Such are our facilities for the attainment of wealth, and such the bounty of divine Providence, that our merchants are as the princes of Tyre. We "have made haste to be rich." Early and late, in season and out of season, the strongest faculties of body and mind, with a directness of purpose, and an energy, an intensity of action, have been directed to the acquisition of wealth. *Gold* may well be called the *Moloch* of the land. It is a king whose court none can approach without paying homage. With unblushing effrontery it makes its way to the ballot-box, and gives its impulse to the rough machinery of our popular elections. The Shibboleth of party rings through its halls, and even sworn legislators worship at its altars; and what is worse, *justice*, the last refuge of society, and which should be alike indifferent to the smiles or the frowns, the caprices or the passions of the people; which ought to be independent of every thing but an enlightened and honest conscience, and which ought to be blind to every thing except to "the law and the testimony," pays tribute to the shrine of Mammon. That mischievous maxim that "to the victors belong the spoils," has become embodied in the creed of the nation, and even now threatens to give the death-blow to the republic. These are humiliating admissions; but such, to a lamentable and ill-boding extent, is the character of the American people. We "have made gold our hope, and said to the fine gold, *thou* art our confidence."

Yet who does not see that "riches can not save us in the day of wrath?" Gold can not harmonize our counsels; can not bring back lost opportunities; can not rectify our blunders; can not tell us when, and where, and how to strike the heaviest blow; can not shield us from treachery; and can not impart either the ability or the integrity which the nation calls for. Rather does it stimulate that egotism and peculation which excite suspicion and disturb the confidence of honest men.

This pomp of riches, this boast of national wealth, what is it? How vain is it to array the mines of California and the vaults of Wall Street against an all-pervading Providence! Babylon the great was decked with gold, and precious stones, and pearls; she glorified herself, and lived deliciously; yet her merchant princes wept over her, for in one hour her great riches came to naught. No, we are not entitled to victory because *we have the longest purse.* There must be another will, another power, and the utterance of another voice. No: "let not the rich man glory in his riches."

If you ask *why we may not glory in these things,* the answer is easily given. Nations may not be governed by other principles of morality than those which ought to control the individuals who compose them. We have little respect *for the man* whose measures and conduct are controlled by the spirit of self-aggrandizement. Deeply rooted as this spirit is in the human heart, and all-pervading as is its influence, it is "out and out" the spirit of evil. It makes men, and not patriots; it may make conquerors, but not heroes; it forms the victims of an ambition which grasps at empire, but not just men ruling in the fear of God.

3

Nothing disarms its fury or arrests its violence. And it is just as bad in *nations* as in *men*. It is less unseemly, because it has the mien of greatness; it is less ignoble and condemned, because it is more splendid. It seems to savor of a generous patriotism, but it sets up only the phantom of national glory. It amuses and dazzles, and the giddy and unthinking follow it as they do the path of the meteor.

The "Most High, who ruleth among the children of men," *forbids* this spirit. "Cursed is the man," says he, "that trusteth in man, and maketh flesh his arm." He calls it idolatry when we thus "sacrifice to our own net, and burn incense to our own drag." It is the spirit which he hates, and is determined to abase. There is no lesson in his Word more obvious than this. There is nothing in his government of the world which he is so set on humbling as this pride of man. He has read the lesson so often in order that "no flesh should glory in his presence," and he will read it again from the stormy sea, from the angry heavens, and from the lurid battle-field. It is this self-glorying spirit which banished angels from their thrones; which kindled the flames of Sodom; which overthrew Pharaoh and his hosts in the Red Sea; and which precipitated the Sauls, the Cyruses, the Alexanders, the Cæsars, the Alarics, the Genghis Khans, and the Napoleons of our earth to an untimely and ignoble grave. Yet Nebuchadnezzar was scarcely more intoxicated with the pomp and pride of royalty when he walked in his palace and said, "Is not this great Babylon which I have built by the might of my power and the honor of my majesty?" than has been and is the proud and vaunting spirit of the American people. We are an arrogant nation, prompt to defy the world in arms, and to challenge all comparison with other lands. Instead of moving on in our course courageously and faithfully, meekly and in the fear of God, and fulfilling our mission so as to establish the truth that man is capable of self-government, our hearts have been lifted up, we have walked loftily, rushing in the pursuit of greatness, reckless and extravagant, and confident of our resources. "Young America," the special genius of the age, a conceited, brave, impetuous youth, revering nothing, fearing nothing, has been our idol, and on this altar we have sacrificed not a little of the morals and the true dignity of the nation.

I do not look for the admiration and applause of men in giving utterance to thoughts like these. The theme is one which does not vibrate to the popular ear. Bitter experience may teach us these lessons; but how much wiser, how much safer to "hear the rod, and who hath appointed it," and listen to his voice "now in this accepted time." Let us, then,

II. In the second place, ADVERT TO THE THINGS IN WHICH WE MAY GLORY.

There are other and higher principles of action than those to which we have referred, and we gladly turn to them. They are high and exalted principles, and in alliance with heaven's conflict with the powers of darkness. They are the knowledge, the love, the fear, the will, the favor of the Most High. If I know myself, my object in addressing you is to HONOR THE SUPREME RULER OF THE UNIVERSE, and in this solemn controversy call upon our rulers, our warriors, and my countrymen every where to give glory to the Lord God omnipotent. While "the wise may not glory in their wisdom," nor the mighty in their might, nor the rich in their wealth, there is One in whom they may glory. "*Thus saith the Lord,*" Let him that glorieth glory in this,

that he UNDERSTANDETH AND KNOWETH ME,
THAT I AM THE LORD THAT EXERCISE LOVING-
KINDNESS, JUDGMENT, AND RIGHTEOUSNESS IN
THE EARTH; FOR IN THESE THINGS DO I DELIGHT,
SAITH THE LORD. Let us amplify these in-
structive and precious thoughts.

Thus saith the Lord, "Let him that glorieth glory in this, that he UNDERSTANDETH AND
KNOWETH ME." It is a humiliating fact that so
little is known of God in the very world which
was made by him, and which is upheld and
governed by his omnipotent hand. Men "do
not like to retain God in their knowledge."
Though he is every where present, and more
interested in them, and they have more to do
with him, and he with them, than any other
being in the universe, yet they say, "How
doth God know? Can he judge through the
dark cloud?"

It is emphatically the sin of nations that, in
prosperity and adversity, in peace and in war,
they think so little of God, and in their counsels, their public documents, their victories,
and their defeats, are so slow of heart to acknowledge and honor his supremacy. Yet is
"the Lord, whose name is jealous, a jealous
God." He forms a just estimate of his own

character, claims, and prerogatives, and justly
requires that a fitting regard be paid to them
by all the nations of the earth. He can not
be indifferent to their treatment of him any
more than he can deny himself. If the dispensations of his providence are often dark
and mysterious, and often contravene the designs, arrangements, and expectations of men,
it is that they "may know that he is the Lord
in the midst of the earth." He would wake
up their attention to the reality of his being,
and bring his character and government distinctly before their minds. Many are the pe-
riods in the history of the world when these
great realities have forced themselves upon
the consideration of the unthinking nations.
Many is the epoch in our own national history when rulers and subjects have been con-
strained to go beyond their ordinary convictions, and been made to feel, and *feel deeply*,
that there is a Power above us. We may
well give this truth an abiding lodgment in
our hearts. With all our wisdom, all our
prowess, and all our wealth, there is One who
"increaseth the nations and destroyeth them,
and who enlargeth the nations and straiten-
eth them again;" who controls the material

and the moral, the civil and the religious, in and by all accomplishing his own benevolent and holy ends. We shall never feel as we ought, nor conduct the great and solemn work in which we are employed as it ought to be conducted, until we feel our dependence on God, and lay ourselves in humble prostration at his feet. " Shall the axe boast itself against him that heweth therewith ? or shall the saw magnify itself against him that shaketh it ? as if the rod should shake itself against them that lift it up, or as if the staff should lift up itself as if it were no wood !"

There is no lesson more important at such a day of rebuke as this than that we " UN-DERSTAND AND KNOW HIM"—HIM, the Eternal and Infinite One, who was, and is, and is to come, when the nations are dissolved, and the heavens and the earth have passed away— *Him* who, while time is measuring off and, in its rapid and silent progress transforming all created things, remains the same, yesterday, to-day, and forever—*Him* whose immensity is as unbounded as his being, who comprises all, and is comprised by none ; who sees alike in the thickest darkness and in the bright sun-light, and from whom there is no retreat, on

land or sea, in heaven or hell—*Him*, the all-
powerful God, the Lord of Hosts, who holds
creation in his hands, before whom the flow-
er of Lebanon fades away, and the beauty of
Bashan and Carmel languish, and at whose
command the sun and the moon stand still,
that kings and heroes may be broken in pieces
as a potter's vessel—*Him* from whom and to
whom are all things, who holdeth the waters
in the hollow of his hand, and turneth the
heart of kings as the rivers of water are turned.

In such a one may we glory, not only for
these attributes of greatness, but, more than all,
for the *moral properties of his nature*. "I,"
says he, "am the Lord which exercise *loving-
kindness, judgment, and righteousness* in the
earth." His greatness fills our minds with
reverence and awe; his loving-kindness at-
tracts our love and confidence; it charms us;
we glory in it; it is emphatically the glory of
his nature. There would be no beauty, no
loveliness in his character, were there no kind
and benevolent affections. These are his
adornment; without them, he would be but "a
consuming fire." And these, marvelous to be
revealed to such a sinning and abject world

as this, are the precursors and heralds of his
providence, publishing as they go that "he *is*
good and *does* good, and that his tender mer-
cies are over all his works." If we glory in
him we shall be more like him, and not carry
a bitter and malignant, or revengeful spirit
even to the field of battle. This is not the
spirit of the God of battles. Every righteous
war is a benevolent war; and when its great
and good ends are attained, it sheathes the
sword.

We may glory in him also because he exercises *judgment* in the earth. "Behold, therefore, the goodness and the severity of God."
We sometimes look abroad upon the world
in which we dwell, and wonder at the disasters which befall it. But we are creatures
of a day, and know nothing. When we think
of his *loving-kindness*, we may not forget that
"verily there is a God that *judgeth* in the
earth." They are impressive views of the
divine character that are often manifested in
the dispensations of a punitive providence.
Holy angels and holy men, the Church in
heaven and the Church in earth, would be
thrown into deep confusion and dismay if
they did not know that "justice and judgment

are the habitation of his throne." He is their refuge and strength, and they look to him for protection and safety, to plead and maintain their cause, to oppose, and confound, and destroy their enemies, because he "exercises *judgment* in the earth." They direct their supplications to him, and "by terrible things in righteousness does he answer them." His benevolent designs, his gracious promises can not be accomplished without affecting judgments. There are crises in the history of nations when an interposing and punitive providence is necessary to his own wise arrangements. We may be brought low, but our help and our hope are in Him who not only exercises loving-kindness, but *judgment* in the earth. If there are those who wrong us, sooner or later they will complete the measure of their arrogance, and be made to feel the weight of his omnipotent hand.

And what may more increase our hope and confidence is the assurance that he "exercises *righteousness* in the earth." He is quick to discern what is right and what is wrong. His moral rectitude was never tarnished by his approbation of wrong-doing. "He is a Rock; his work is perfect; a God of truth and without iniquity, *just and right is he.*" Every true patriot desires nothing but what is right for his country. If he adopts the prayer of the Psalmist against his enemies, "Destroy thou them, O God; let them fall by their own counsels; cast them out in the multitude of their transgressions, for they have rebelled against thee," it is because their appeal is founded on the divine righteousness. Under the righteous government of the Most High, wicked men and wicked nations may expect to be overtaken by the divine judgments, and in their bold and impious wickedness to be caught in their own snare. He will plead his own cause. As the Judge of the earth, he will "lift up himself and render a reward to the proud."

They are no local or partial interests that he looks upon, but the great interests of the Church and the world. His loving-kindness, his judgment, and his righteousness stand firm; they stand upright and abreast, and, through the redemption of his Son, in undisturbed harmony and in unsullied beauty. We wonder most at his loving-kindness; yet we may not be disappointed if even justice is meted out to the nations of the earth, and so conspicuously that the righteous shall adore the hand that lifts them up, and the wicked shall feel the blow that crushes them—so conspicuously that "the Lord alone shall be exalted in that day."

In these things we may glory. On these we may rely. These we are under sacred obligations to honor. If you ask *how* we shall honor them, I answer by distinctly recognizing them; by our obedience to God's commands; by our reverence for his name and his institutions; by our submission to his will, and by our regard and solicitude for his kingdom of truth and righteousness, peace and joy. And do you ask *why* we ought to glory in these things? I answer, Heaven glories in them, and earth may well glory in them. Heaven long ago began the ascription, "Great and marvelous are thy works, Lord God Almighty; just and true are thy ways, O thou King of Saints!" And the earth may well respond to the ascription. God himself glories in just such weighty realities as these. Mercy and justice — justice, without which wickedness is sure to be triumphant; mercy, without which we all perish—"in these things do I delight, saith the Lord." This, too, is the proper business, the true honor and blessedness of man. When God called the American people from lands of tyranny and persecution; when he drove out the heathen before them, and gave them this fair land for a possession to themselves and their children; when he carried them triumphantly through the conflict which resulted in establishing us one of the independent nations of the earth; when he gave us a Constitution and a government so fitted to our wants, our enlargement, and our prosperity, it was that we might honor him, and promote the wise and benevolent ends he had in view in assigning to us this honored place among the kingdoms of this world. This is our high calling; and we may despair of accomplishing it if we ignore our dependence upon him and our trust in him. He is worthy of this confidence, and requires us to cast ourselves upon him for the accomplishment of his designs and our vocation. Independently of him, we do but rush upon our own destruction. Look the world over, read the history of the past, and you will find that the happiest nations and· the most honored were those whose character and laws, whose liberty and order the most

exalted the God of heaven. The foundations
of this government were laid by him; he took
the work into his own hands; it was settled
and arranged by him; and when it was com-
pleted it was a work worthy of its divine Au-
thor. And now that it has enjoyed such
marked tokens of his favor, and we are called on to defend and perpetuate its existence
and its heaven-imparted blessings, shall we
not look to him to plan for us and to provide
for us still, and, as we address ourselves to
coming dangers, fix our eyes upon "the pillar
of cloud by day" and of "fire by night?"
Then, this conflict over, and union and peace
restored to this convulsed land, we shall know,
and the nations of the earth will know, what
a God there is in heaven. The world will
know that he hath gotten to himself a great
name, and that he is the Head and glory of
these states, and the "rewarder of them that
diligently seek him."

Such are the principles by which, as a nation, we ought to be governed. They are true
principles; and, like all moral truth, are the
source of high and noble impulses. They are
motives which form the character of every
good man, every good ruler, every good army.

They are principles of action which are effective, full of energy, and which can endure reverses and become stronger by defeat, and which no changes of fortune and no discouragement can eradicate. They will not become giddy by victory, nor will they expire in the confusion of battle and amid garments rolled in blood. They will not move with the multitude simply because the multitude move, but only as it moves right. They will not change to time-serving and trickishness, but will stand stable and firm. They will not blow up the flame of war without reason, nor will they cry " Peace, peace," when pride and contention, animosity and strife, wrong and wrong-doers, are breaking up the integrity of the nation, and overturning the harmony and prosperity of the world. They are agitating principles only against evil, coalescing and combining with every element of goodness and rectitude. There is no safety for a nation that despises or dishonors them. Patriotism is never so pure, so exalted, so to be relied on as when it springs from moral principle, and is founded in affectionate reverence for God. " It is better to trust in the Lord than to have confidence in men; it is better to trust in the Lord than to have confidence in princes." It is his own declaration, "Them that honor me I will honor, and they that despise me shall be lightly esteemed."

With all the profusion of the divine bounty scattered over the land, this year 1861 has been, and is, a year of unparalleled severity to the American people. We are now amid the calamities of civil war. Portions of the land are the theatre of violence and blood: carnage and desolation have swept over their fields and their villages, and humanity weeps. Though we ourselves are at a distance from this work of death, we sympathize in its paralyzing influence through all the departments of life and business, converting, as it does, seats of industry and joyous homes into boding silence, restless anxiety, and bitter tears. Nor may we predict what will be on the morrow. No mortal eye can see what reverses we may meet with, nor under what strokes of a righteous and chastening Providence we may be called to bleed.

When the first indications of this conflict made their appearance, all my prepossessions, as is well known, were with the Southern States. If their leading statesmen had conducted themselves like men; if the ministers of the Gospel and their churches had conducted themselves like Christians and as friends of peace — for myself, I would have been the advocate of some amicable arrangement rather than have been forced to the arbitrament of the sword. But when, instead of this, I hear so few kind words, and these suppressed by violence or fear; when crafty politicians, eager for fame, and panting for place and power, blind and enslave the minds of the people; when I learn that this secession was preconcerted and determined on in years gone by, and was only "biding its time," and that the time and the occasion for it were all arranged, and the signal given and the blow struck for causes over which the South not only had entire control, but itself created; when I read the ordinance of secession itself, severing the tie that bound the people of the United States together so prosperously and happily, and all because the Slave States had for a time lost their supremacy; when, to insure this severance, men high in office, in the cabinet, in the army, in the navy, at home and abroad, became false to their oaths of citizenship and of office, spoilers of the public treas-

ury and traitors to their country; when, in the
phrensy of their rebellion, they form a government, seize our forts and arsenals, our national ships and our navy-yards, appropriate the
government property, dishonor and insult our
national flag, and by an armed force threaten
the very city of our solemnities, and all this
when the government of the nation has been
virtually in the hands of the South for the
greater part of our national existence, and that when
from the adoption of the Federal Constitution
down to the repeal of the Missouri Compro-
mise the North has made concession upon
concession without satisfying the demands
of her exacting neighbors—when I see these
things, my convictions are strong that we have
reached the limit beyond which forbearance
may not be extended. Who will complain
that we grasped the sword? Strong as have
been my predilections for the South, and decided as my views still are that on her return
to her loyalty she is entitled to equal rights
and immunities with the North, I have not
been able to see, nor do I now see, the justice,
the equity of her demands. We regard the
act of secession, so causeless, so rash, so fratricidal, so ruthless, as unequaled in wicked-

ness. I do not know that the history of the world records a ' more criminal procedure. After what I have said on a former occasion, it is needless for me to enlarge on this theme. Proof upon proof has been multiplied in the daily and weekly journals, in the quarterly reviews and periodicals, and in discourses from the pulpit, many of them written with great candor and great ability, of the fallacy, the political heresy of the doctrine that every state possesses the reserved right of withdrawing at pleasure from the federal compact. Concede this, and we have no Union, no government, no nation ; secession abolishes the national constitution and subverts its government.

We should have no difference of opinion as to the part which the Church of God, in her organized capacity, ought to pursue in this matter if we are once united on this one question. If the question were a mere political one, and had no moral bearings, we might hesitate. If it were an open question, we might hesitate. As Presbyterians, and guided not merely by the convictions of conscience, but by the decisions of the assembled Church, we regard secession not merely as a "political blunder," but as crime, as sin against God and man. If the Church of God may not bear her testimony against such wickedness, what is the design and object of her organization? Is it that her light may shine, or that she may put it under a bushel? If human governments "frame iniquity by a law;" if, for example, they legalize profanity, dueling, the slave-trade, Sabbath-breaking, theft, murder, must the Church, as such, be silent, simply because sins like these have the seal of her country's legislation? We have not so learned Christ. There is no form of wickedness against which she is not bound to enter her solemn protest. Christians are bound to do so as Christians. Sessions, presbyteries, synods, and the General Assembly are bound to do so by their public acts. We do not understand the logic, the morality, or the Presbyterianism of imposing silence on ecclesiastical judicatories in matters of such grave moment to truth and righteousness. I would be slow to put into the hands of Congregationalists and Independents so heavy a weapon against our own ecclesiastical organization as to affirm that when "political questions rise to the sphere of morals and religion," the rule of action is not to be sought in the law of God. The *protest* of the minority of the last General Assembly against the scriptural action of that body upon this subject is before the world; and, notwithstanding the authority of the source from which it proceeded, its sophistry and weakness are by this time sufficiently apparent. When loyalty to our country is acknowledged to be "a moral and religious duty," and when the "right of the Assembly to enjoin this duty on the ministers and churches under its care" is unequivocally avowed, it appears to us that the Protestants themselves decide this great moral question; and it is but miserable quibbling by which they would traverse their own declaration. I crave to know if the Church of God has no right to her deliverance of the truth as it is in Jesus on such a question as this. We desire no stronger language than the words of this protest itself. "If the state pass any laws contrary to the law of God, then it is the duty of the Church, to whom God has committed the great work of asserting and maintaining his truth and will, to protest and remonstrate." The simple question is, Is this secession of the South morally right? If not, it is an egregious wrong; and that

man does not honor the name of Presbyterian
who is unwilling to say so. Thanks to the
great Head of the Church, this cautious skep-
ticism taints the minds of but few in the midst
of us. The history of the Church of Scotland
and of our own Church furnishes emphatic
records of the right and duty of the Church
of God to warn those under their care against
the wicked legislation of human governments.
In other ages it was her privilege, in defiance
of the sword and the fagot, to assert the authority of her great Head over all human laws.
We live in an age of the world too far ad-
vanced in civil and religious liberty, and too
imperative in its demands on the moral courage of good men, to be restrained from utter-
ing the truth in plain language.   And, if we
mistake not, those, and especially those ministers of the Gospel who question the correct-
ness of these views, will be found, both in their
preaching and in their prayers, to be exceed-
ingly wary, if not *non-committal*, upon the
great wickedness of the Southern rebellion.
Probe them, and, with some noble exceptions,
you will find them rotten at the core.*

* Among these exceptions the editor of the Danville Re-
view holds an honorable place.

The action of the last General Assembly meant to decide the question to what government the allegiance of Presbyterians as citizens is due. They meant to decide the question that, in this land, it is primarily due to the United States. When it called upon the churches under its care to strengthen and uphold THE FEDERAL GOVERNMENT, they knew what they were about; and if they did not mean to decide this question, they decided nothing. They rightly called upon the churches even in the rebellious states to protest *against wickedness*, and to lift their voices *against rebellion*. It is puerile to say that they should hesitate in so doing because their action exposed the Southern churches to the frowns of the so-called government of the South. The simple question is, Is the pseudo-government of the South A GOVERNMENT *which is the ordinance of God*, or is it a *wicked revolt* from the "powers that be, and are ordained of God?" If the latter, it was the sacred and most religious duty of Southern ministers to discountenance it, be *the consequences what they may.* What if it did expose them to peril in the cause of truth and righteousness? Is this an anomaly in the history of the Church of God, as though "some strange thing" had happened to her? And I take leave to say, with all frankness, if the *ministers of the Gospel at the South* had not shut their ears against the instructions of God's Word—if they had honestly and earnestly sought to know the truth, and had boldness equal to the exigency, this frightful conflict *would never have desolated the land.* A little firmness on the part of our Southern brethren would have chained "the dogs of war" and saved the country. In my humble judgment, fearful wickedness is attached to the pulpits of the South in this matter. If they had not been given over to great mental blindness, in defiance of all artifice and menaces of perfidious politicians, they would have arrested the hand of the destroyer. The pulpit of the South does not know its power. Does not know its power, did I say? I recall the words. It knows it too well, and has exerted it too systematically. It was among the earliest and boldest preachers of sedition: the course it pursued was rebellion baptized in the waters of the sanctuary. Its ministers are not only rebels, but among the leaders of a rebellion which they might have crushed in the bud. What the issue will be is in the

hands of a wise and almighty Providence.
They have "sown the wind," and it would be
no unusual and no undeserved result if they
"reap the whirlwind." I can excuse the ig-
norant, and even the arrogant, for the part
they have been instigated to tread on this field
of blood, but I can not excuse Christian ministers. I could say something to palliate the
perfidy and intrigue of ambitious statesmen;
but for good men, able men, God's ministers,
knowing as they do that the North asked
nothing, aimed at nothing, and were pursuing
nothing but the supremacy of the laws and
the maintenance of equal rights in every part
of the Union, to stamp upon and tread in the
dust the principles which their and our fathers
secured by so much service and suffering—
for this we have no apology. They are traitors, striking blow after blow upon all that is
vital in the structure of human society; and
not a few of them, in all the sanctity of their
official robes, are *armed* traitors.

War is a fearful remedy, but history teach-
es us that there are greater evils than the
shock of battle. God grant that we may
never learn that the destruction of our Constitution and our Union is a greater evil; that
the loss of our civil and religious liberty is a

greater evil; that a Southern EMPIRE, extend-
ing to Cuba and Mexico, with the slave-trade
as its basis, is not a greater evil; that the ex-
tinction of our national life, in which so many
precious hopes for ourselves, for posterity, for
the world, are bound up, is a greater evil.
We reluctantly take up the sword in defense
of the rich heritage God has given us, and
most cheerfully will we return it to its scab-
bard when this heritage is secure. We feel
no responsibility resting upon us as friends
of the federal government but that of self-de-
fense. In resorting to this stern arbitrament
of the sword, there is fearful responsibility
somewhere. And we call the nations of the
earth to witness—nay, we call the God of nations to witness that, instead of seeking, we
not only did not desire it, we did not expect
it; we were utterly unprepared for it; it came
upon us like the lightning in a midsummer
day. It will be the joy of our hearts and the
thank-offering of our lips to sound the retreat
the moment the voice of rebellion is silent.
We have no bitterness against the South.
We do not wish to reign over them, but to
reign with them, and wish them to reign with
us, and to participate equally with us, as they
ever have done, in all the rights and immuni-

ties of the federal government. This will not satisfy them, and hence the carnage. Their consciences testify where the responsibility rests. No man questions the fact that this fratricidal war took its rise from them; and we are bold to say it did not take its rise from the love of truth and rectitude, nor from the love of God or man. In view of the unmeasured calamities of this contest, its authors have a solemn account to render to themselves, to the God of nations, to the civilized and uncivilized world.

This is the ground on which I stand as an American citizen and as a Christian minister. I have confidence in the rectitude of our cause; I have confidence in the loyalty of the people; I have confidence in the valor of our arms; and I have *confidence in God*. The most depraved and ambitious of our enemies are under his control, to be restrained in their outrageous passions, frustrated in their daring designs, and turned from them to purposes of conciliation and peace. We do not expect miracles from his hand even in a just cause. He has other ways of working, and they are the instrumentalities and agencies of wise counsels, carried into effect by the united energy of the people. It is thus he will make

bare his arm and defend the right. I plead
with my countrymen to give God the throne;
but I am no advocate for the faith that is without works. It was sound theology, sound morals, and true heroism when Cromwell exhort-
ed his soldiers to "trust in God, and keep their
powder dry." Our strength lies not in an in-
active trust in God, but in strong convictions
of right and duty; in unsleeping watchfulness
and undiscouraged effort; in losing sight of
the miserable distinctions of party for the
common weal; in being fellow-workers with
the All-wise, and All-powerful, and Supreme
Ruler in crushing this gigantic and causeless
rebellion. And when this fierce flame has
burnt itself out, or been quenched in showers
of mercy or showers of wrath, we will not
forget who it is that "breaketh the bow, and
cutteth the spear asunder, and burneth the
chariot in the fire."

We have a duty to perform, my countrymen, and we may not be disheartened by dif-
ficulties. It has been well said that "reverses
dishearten only where there is weakness to
be disheartened. Small is the strength, any
where and every where, that can not stand
adversity; and small will it stay, and smaller
will it grow, to the end." We have met with

reverses, but those very reverses have assured us that we have no ground for discouragement. When the ten tribes revolted from the throne of David, Israel did not lose its confidence in God. When our Revolutionary fathers fled before the British cannon and the Indian tomahawk, they did not lose their confidence in God. They were reared and nursed amid reverses, and came from scenes of blood to found this empire of law, order, and liberty. They are looking down upon us to-day, and I seem to hear them say to you and to me, "Hold fast that thou hast; let no man take thy crown."

For myself, I hardly hope to survive this fearful controversy. I love the land which gave me birth, and which is the place of my fathers' and my childrens' sepulchres. I love it as one of the stanch pillars of good government; as the friend and patron of every good word and work; as the soil where the vine that was brought out of Egypt has flourished and filled the land; as destined to herald forth and perpetuate those "years of the right hand of the Most High," when "knowledge, with strength of salvation, shall be the stability of the times." I am sensible we are exposed by our self-confidence. We have stood on an elevation so lofty that it is easy for us to become giddy and have our heads turned. Let us take shame to ourselves, and suppress the flame of turbulent passion and vainglory. If a wise providence designs this war as a school in which the American character is to be burnished and invigorated, it is that we may study and learn those high principles of morality and rectitude which will guide its upward and onward course, and whence it may start afresh on a career of honor to itself and a blessing to the world.

It is with monitions and hopes like these that we hail THIS DAY OF THANKSGIVING AND PRAISE. It is in every view fitting that we make our grateful acknowledgments to the Great Giver for his distinguished goodness toward us during the year. Such health, such plenty, such promptness to anticipate the wants of the poor, even in the midst of all these stagnations of business and commercial embarrassments, demand our thanks. Nor is this all. Does not this rising of a great people in defense of their government demand our thanks? Do not the public proclamations of the chief magistrate of the nation, and of the chief magistrate of our own commonwealth, so beautifully recognizing the claims of the Supreme Ruler, demand our thanks? Does not the official and personal reverence for the God of heaven on the part of the youthful chief of our armies demand our thanks? Do not the suppression of vice, and the encouragements and facilities to Christian worship and moral virtue among our soldiery, and an increasing reverence for the Sabbath among ourselves, demand our thanks? Do not the successes of our arms by sea and by land demand our thanks? Does not the very period in our history in which a righteous Providence has called us to this conflict—a period which, had it been deferred for twenty years, would have seen us a ruined people, and ruined by our own corruptions—a conflict for which, in wealth and numbers, we were never so well prepared, demand our thanks? Does not the state of the world, teeming with events of religious interest, and on the tiptoe of expectation for the downfall of every form of anti-Christ, and the universal spread of the Gospel of the Son of God, demand our thanks? And does not even our present position, arranged and decided by a wise Providence for such an age and state of the world as those we now occupy, inspire hopes and expectations that should fill our hearts with confidence and our lips with praise?

But, while this is the hour of thanksgiving, it becomes us to be humble as well as thankful. It may be doubted whether there is any true gratitude where there is no humility. Humility is the breath of gratitude, because we are so unworthy and ill-deserving; gratitude is humility's song, because the God of nations so delights in exercising loving-kindness, judgment, and righteousness in the earth. Let us therefore bow in humble gratitude before the eternal throne, and, while we discern streams of light in the cloud that hangs over us, commit this conflict and its issues to *Him*. Let us take heed lest we think of ourselves more highly than we ought to think, and lose sight of Him by whom kings reign and princes decree justice. It is the great God who is speaking to us. Let us give glory to Him before he cause darkness, and our feet stumble upon the dark mountains. The wisdom of the wise, the power of the mighty, the wealth of the rich, consist in feeling their dependence upon Him, in acknowledging their obligations to Him, in giving Him the glory to whom all glory belongs.